Time Management For Girls

A Quick Help Book

A. T. Sorsa

Copyright © 2011 A. T. Sorsa

All rights reserved.

ISBN: 1461135281

ISBN-13: 978-1461135289

Content

CHAPTER 1: TIME DOES NOT PLAY FAVORITES 1

CHAPTER 2: WHAT IS TIME MANAGEMENT? 5

CHAPTER 3: WHY TIME MANAGEMENT? ... 8

CHAPTER 4: GET ORGANIZED! 13

CHAPTER 5: THE GIRL WHO INVENTED THE TIME MACHINE 16

CHAPTER 6: TIME MANAGEMENT TECHNIQUES AND METHODS 28

CHAPTER 7: TASK LISTS – WHAT ARE THEY? 36

CHAPTER 8: PRIORITIZE YOUR TASKS! 40

CHAPTER 9: LEARN TO SAY "NO!" 45

CHAPTER 10: GOOD HABITS 47

ABOUT THE AUTHOR 49

BOOKS BY A.T. SORSA 50

CHAPTER 1:
TIME DOES NOT PLAY FAVORITES

Everyone has the same 24-hour day to do our chores and tasks. It is just 1,440 minutes for all the daily tasks. It's not so much when you have homework and other chores to do, and you want to play, too.

Time flies!

There are not so many hours in a day if you waste your time and procrastinate!

There are not enough hours after school if you don't organize and manage your time. You know how many hours you are at school. After school, you have only a certain amount of time to study, to do your homework, to play and do your hobbies.

STUDY AND PLAY TIME

If you plan ahead, you will gain a sense of satisfaction with how you use your hours.

You need to change your habits of what to do and when to do it if you want to manage your time better.

It's easy if you start paying attention of what you do and when you do and what you need to do today, tomorrow and this week.

SLEEP TIME

You also need sleep in order to be awake and alert at school the next day. Sleep causes your body to refresh and heal, and you will be ready to face new challenges the next day when you wake up.

Good night sleep includes at least eight hours continuous, uninterrupted sleep. Some people need more sleep, and some can do with fewer hours.

If you don't sleep enough, then you will be sleepy and tired all day. You will yawn and rub your eyes to stay awake. You will not be able to concentrate if you are tired. Your learning abilities are not that good when you are tired.

CHAPTER 2:
WHAT IS TIME MANAGEMENT?

Time management includes the skill of how to better use your time. These skills are for example, setting objectives, making lists, dividing tasks into smaller tasks and prioritizing activities, and so on. These skills help us to manage our use of time.

Time management will make you learn how to manage your own behavior, actions and tasks.

You learn these different time management skills to improve your performance and to do more with the time you have. Time management and planning ahead helps you to accomplish your tasks on time.

Some of us seem to accomplish more and seem to be better at time management than others. Maybe they are born with good planning skills, or maybe they have learned how to use their time and how to plan ahead. They have also learned to appreciate result of their planning.

Maybe they have learned discipline and know that wasting time does not get you anywhere and success comes with hard work, effort, and consistency.

CHAPTER 3:
WHY TIME MANAGEMENT?

Why time management is so important?

Why is it good to organize?

Why is it a great idea to divide tasks to different task lists and prioritize them?

Here are some reasons why:

If you want to get better grades at school, you need to learn to manage your time and organize.

If you have trouble finishing your tasks or your chores at home, you need to learn to manage your time and prioritize your daily tasks: which tasks need to be finished first, and which ones that need to wait until the first tasks are done.

If you want to be better in any sport activities, you need to learn discipline and to manage your time.

If you want to learn new skills, then you need to first have time to learn the new skills, and that means… organize and prioritize your tasks!!

Also, when you learn time management, you develop yourself and you have new organizational skills that can make you to be a better student and also better in other chores that require similar organizational and time management skills. These skills will help you in the future when you look for a job, too.

But, if you say that this is not what you want, then think again!

Think about your dreams, and what do you like to do: Do you want to be the best cheerleader in your state? Do you want to be the number one swimmer in your state? Do you want to be the best ballet dancer in the world? Do you want to be an artist, a writer or an actor?

When you picture yourself doing the things you like to do, then you know that you need time to do that. In order to get more time to do the tasks you really like to do, you need to organize and prioritize all of your tasks… you need time management skills to apply the appropriate amount of time in each task!

Anything you want to do requires time.

You can't get better grades at school just by wishing you would. The tooth fairy won't leave the good grades under your pillow. The Sandman won't bring you the right test answers in your dream. The twinkling star outside your window, won't grant you the better grades. Santa Claus won't leave the report card with A-grades under the Christmas tree.

Getting better grades means hard work and discipline: You must listen to your teacher, make notes, finish your homework and projects, understand what you are doing and prepare yourself for the next school day. That is called self-discipline. You do things what you necessarily don't like to do in order to be able to do something fun.

The self-discipline, managing your time, organizing and prioritizing your tasks will allow you reach your dream goals: getting better grades at school, being a better athlete or an artist, or whatever you want to be within a reasonable amount of time.

CHAPTER 4:
GET ORGANIZED!

Your parents and grandparents have had different methods in organizing their time. Time management and organization methods have changed a lot over the years and generations.

Your great-grandparents used paper notes to remind themselves to do different tasks. These paper notes helped to remind of all the tasks needed to be done on a daily basis.

Your grandparents did not have computers and they did not use the calendar on a cell phone or on a computer. They used the clocks and watches to remind them what to do and where to go.

They also used appointment notebooks to write down their meetings and tasks. These notebooks and watches helped to set daily and weekly goals.

You will hear your parents talking about cell phone reminders to do something on a specific day or at a specific time.

Your parents and older siblings probably also use planner and calendar -applications in their desk computer, cell phone, palm computer or laptop to remind them of all the tasks they need to accomplish in a day. These applications are also called personal organizers. These applications help to clarify the priorities and values of different tasks and activities. It also helps to set goals on a daily or weekly basis.

CHAPTER 5:
THE GIRL WHO INVENTED THE TIME MACHINE

Once upon a time there was a little girl who had trouble with her time management. Her name was Timmie.

Timmie had trouble getting her chores done in time. She forgot to do her homework at least once a week, and got F-grades because she never returned her homework to her teacher.

Every morning Timmie was late. She was always the last one running after the bus or panting inside the bus after running from home to the bus stop. Many mornings she missed the bus and had to go back and ask her parents to take her to school: "Mom! I missed the bus again! Can one of you take me to school this morning?"

"Oh no! Not again!" Timmie's mother and father sighed together.

Timmie was desperate. She just could not understand what was wrong with her. She started doing her chores but then she saw an interesting television show, or her friend called, or she started playing with her dolls. The time flied and Timmie had again used all her spare time playing, chatting with her friends and watching television. Now, it was time to go to bed.

Timmie decided that this could not go on. She had to do something to improve her time management and organizational skills.

Next weekend Timmie went to the garage and started building a time machine out of pieces of scrap metal, old sofa, her father's tools and his volt meter to measure electrical potential difference between two points in an electric circuit, her mother's hairdryer, an old television, a broken toaster, lots of duct tape, screws and bolts, and her big brother's bike for building a generator.

It took Timmie all day to finish her time machine – project.

Timmie was exhausted after a long day of work, but she was very proud of the new time machine when it was ready.

Timmie was only eight years old and had already built a time machine. She was a genius!

Timmie thought that when everybody would hear about her successful invention, she would earn millions of dollars and maybe she would not have to go to school after that. She decided that she would give some of her money to her parents so they would not have to work either. She was not so sure if she would give any money to her older brother because he always teased her. Timmie's brother pulled her hair, hid her cat inside the dryer, and he had also hid a frog inside her backpack.

Timmie thought that after inventing time machine she would not have to go to school or to work. Maybe she would have to go to school to learn the maintenance of the time machine, and how to invest her money. But otherwise, why would she have to go to school if she was already rich and famous inventor?!

This is what Timmie's time machine looked like:

Timmie decided to try her machine right away. She set all the three clocks to a different time, and then she sat inside on the old couch and turned the knobs and pulled the steering sticks. She was ready to go back in time to the previous Monday when she had not returned her homework. She waited and waited.
Nothing happened.

Then Timmie had an idea: What if the time has changed? She thought: I just don't know it because I'm inside the time machine! I better go and check from my mom what time it is now!

"Mom! What day it is?" Timmie shouted when she ran inside.

"Timmie, you should know that it is Saturday because you are not at school today. It's your day off," Timmie's mother answered.

Timmie was so disappointed. She had thought that her machine would work and she would be able to fix her homework by travelling back in time. Now she realized that if she wanted to do her homework and return them on time, she would have to concentrate and not be distracted. She would have to learn to set up the alarm clock in the morning in order to wake up on time. She would have to leave her home in time in order to be on time for the bus. There were no shortcuts. It was all up to her. Nobody else could make her be in time and be organized.

After that weekend, Timmie was never late from school. She never missed her school bus, and she never forgot to return her homework on time.

This is how she succeeded in her time management project: Timmie used task lists and prioritized her tasks. She also used highlighters, sticky notes and colorful flags to mark important parts in the books she read.

Then she tried the weekly and monthly planners, which made her time management even more easier.

Timmie made lots of notes.

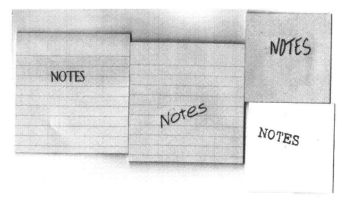

She also had two alarm clocks so that she would not miss going to school in time and would not miss her bus.

Timmie had a folder for all her homework and other school papers to put in her backpack.

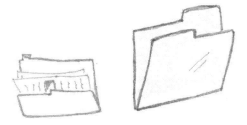

Timmie arranged his folder according to the subject: Math papers to Math folder, Earth Science -papers to Earth Science – folder, and so on.

Timmie had notebooks and extra pencils for school.

By using her folder, Timmie was able to keep her backpack organized and neat. She had a pencil case for her pencils and erasers so that they would not get lost in her backpack.

This is what Timmie's backpack looked like:

Timmie had a big wall calendar to show her the whole month and she could plan ahead what home tasks she had to do and when she had to do them.

But the big wall calendar was not good enough for Timmie. She had trouble remembering to mark down the important tasks and deadlines to her wall calendar. Therefore, Timmie got herself a small weekly planner to take with her and mark down important dates during the school day, too.

She put little flags on the side of the planner to mark down some important deadlines and tasks to be finished. She wrote sticky notes that she could transfer to her wall calendar at home.

This is what Timmie's planner looked like: She had flags to mark important pages in her calendar and also important test days. She had sticky notes to tell her what specific task she had to remember that week.

The next pages will show you how Timmie finally managed to get organized. They will tell you more about Timmie's time management techniques and methods.

CHAPTER 6:
TIME MANAGEMENT TECHNIQUES AND METHODS

Time management includes efficiency in doing your work, like reading and doing your homework. Learning and studying is more than just doing the mandatory homework and projects.

Summarize
Summarize what you have read in your own words; for instance, write down the characters and the plot of the book you just finished. This will help you to save time when you can just look up your notes when you are answering the questions of the book.

Take notes
Take notes of the books you are reading. Taking notes while you read the books helps you to recall the important issues and also answer the questions later on.

Use sticky notes and flags
Do your own sticky notes of the important issues for a quick review or reminder. Colored notes in between book can tell you about the subject, what was important in the chapter. You can even write your own conclusions on a sticky note!

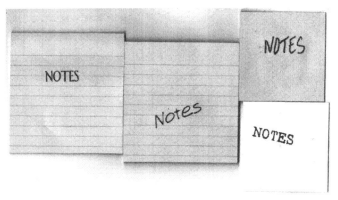

Sticky notes are good reminders! If you need to take something with you to school the next day, then write yourself a sticky note and place it on your mirror or place it so that you will see it the next morning before you go to the school bus.

The **colorful flags** on the page can even tell different issues: red = most important, yellow = interesting to know, blue = key topic, and so on. You can decide the color code yourself. You can write a topic on these flags, and use different sizes of flags. Flagging allows you to set up your own study routines and style.

Make it fun! Color your school day and books with flags, sticky notes and highlighters!

It will be more interesting for you to follow up how your color coding and notes work out, and how your time management improves in time.

Use highlighters!

Why highlighters are important at school?

A highlighter can save time. When you have a lengthy chapter to read, simply highlighting the important parts of the text can make it easier to go over the information later and learn quicker. As you know learning requires repeating, and thus, finding the important information faster saves you time. It's a great way to manage your time!!

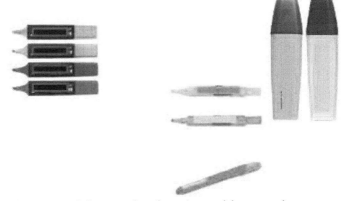

If you are doing a school project with your classmates, then you can highlight the most important parts of the topic and ensure that at least the most important parts are covered in the project. However, if you want to conserve your book for the next student then do not write or highlight the book but use flags and sticky notes instead for your own notes.

There are many sizes of highlighters from thin to thick, combos with pen and highlighter, erasable highlighters, and even highlighters with flags. Choose what is best for you and make it fun!

Don't overdo highlighting because if you underline every sentence in a book, it will start looking messy! That's not the goal! The goal is to save time by making it easier for you to find the important parts of the text by highlighting them with colors.

Use **calendar** to keep track of your projects, homework, chores and tests! The calendar will help you to keep track of days and how many days you have left for a certain deadline, like for instance, the next test.

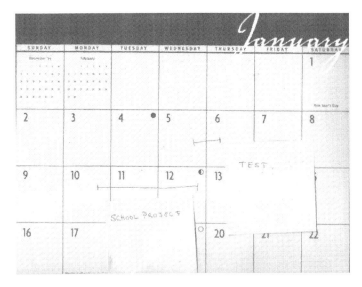

You can draw lines to visualize how many days you need for a certain task, or how much time there is until you have the test.

Use the sticky notes to remind you of important events or tasks to do!

In addition to a wall calendar, use smaller **planners** to mark down important dates and tasks!

Keep extra pencils, pens and erasers with you just in case you lose or misplace one, or if the ink dries out, or the lead breaks.

Use **notebooks** for extra notes!

CHAPTER 7:
TASK LISTS – WHAT ARE THEY?

A task list is **a things-to-do list**. You map out things what you need to do. It is a list of chores to be completed in a day. It's like an inventory in a grocery store: the manager needs to know what is in the store in order to sell it.

Some people like task list. They like to see how many different tasks they have to do in a certain amount of time. Task lists are additional help to keep track of your time and to help you organize and prioritize your tasks.

A task list will you to remember things, to divide them in to smaller tasks and to prioritize what needs to be done immediately and what can wait until the most important tasks are completed first.

You can have more than one list.
But you don't have to have more than one list.

It's up to you if you like to divide your tasks to several lists. You might find out that one list is enough for you.

If you decide to do many task lists and prioritize your list according to your tasks then that might help you keep track of your time and your tasks.

You can have **an A task list** of the most important things that needs to be done immediately. You can also have **B task list, C task list, D task list, and X task list** for the less important tasks.

When you have finished one task, then cross it off of your task list:

~~My task #1~~

Or check it:

DONE! You are ready to move on!

It is important that you cross off the task that you just finished off or check it, because then you can see your progress. You'll also see how many tasks you have completed. Crossing of a task after finishing it will give you satisfaction and motivation to go on. You will see how there are less and less undone tasks on your to-do –lists. Seeing the finished tasks will encourage you to continue to work hard and keep up with your tasks.

CHAPTER 8: PRIORITIZE YOUR TASKS!

You need to certain tasks the same day. Select the tasks that that need to be done right away or the same day. That is you're **A task list**.

```
A list

1. Task
2. Task
3. Task
4. ...
```

There are also task, like your homework, that needs to be returned by certain day. These tasks are graded and assessed by the date when they are returned. Those tasks can be **A, B or C task lists'** tasks depending on how much time you have to complete your homework.

Your B task list's tasks are the tasks that you need to do within 2-3 days. Not right away! Not tonight! Not today!

Your C task list's tasks are the things that you need to do within 4-7 days. You don't need to do these today or tomorrow or even day after that. These can wait!

Your D task list's tasks are your weekend tasks when you don't have school, and when you have more time to do other chores than just homework.

There are things that you can postpone. These you can write on **your X task list**. X task list is your "**nice to do" –list.** These X task list's tasks are nice to do when you have time but it is not within the next 7 days and maybe not even during the next weekend…maybe during your spring break or summer vacation. These tasks can be something special, like for instance, you plan a trip for your next summer vacation with your family.

Now you have all your five lists ready: A, B, C, D and X-task lists.

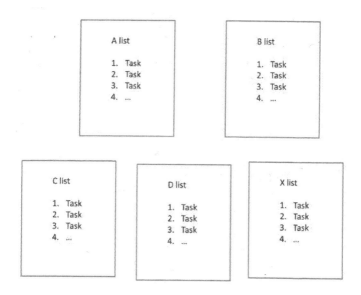

Do you think you have too much to handle now?

Don't worry.

Don't panic even if your lists look long!

Don't drop everything.

Don't pull your hair even if the task list is long!

You can do a step at a time or a chore at a time!

Don't procrastinate!

Don't think a critical task will get done by itself or during your spare time. Remember to schedule your free time, too. Schedule your free time like 3-4 pm after school. You need to take some time off and to relax.

Learn to estimate your tasks. This estimate will improve with practice. You can guess how long a task will take time with or without interruptions. After you have finished the task, write down how long did it take to finish and did you have any interruptions or not.

CHAPTER 9: LEARN TO SAY "NO!"

You can't do everything in a day. You need to learn to tell yourself and other people that you don't have time to do it now. It's okay to say "NO!" sometimes.

> NO!
> I have homework to do.
> I can't do it tonight.
> I can do it tomorrow.

Learn to ask for more time to do your chores at home if you have too much to do on you're a-list.

Also, when you ask for more time, you will show that you know when you can do that task if not now.

If you promise to do it another day, then you will have to keep your promise – otherwise, nobody will believe you next time.

The time you extend from one task takes away time from the following tasks.

Good time management also requires knowing your own limits: what you can do and how much time you need to finish your tasks. If you know you don't have enough time to complete your task in required time then you better communicate that right away. It will show that you know your skills, how much you can do, and it also shows that you can assess yourself and your capabilities.

CHAPTER 10: GOOD HABITS

Keep your school stuff, like your books, pencils, notes, and so on, in one zone in your room. Dedicate that one area for school. That makes it easier for you to find your school stuff.

Efficient study time usually is around 30 minutes. Use breaks when studying! Take 15-20 minutes breaks. The older you get the longer time you can study efficiently.

Have healthy snacks, like apples, bananas, sandwiches, milk and orange juice.

Don't keep radio or television on when you study. The programs can interrupt your concentration, and you will lose time.

Remember to exercise and play, too! One hour a day keeps you healthy and energized!

ABOUT THE AUTHOR

The author has a PhD degree from an AASCB-accredited university. She has studied several subjects, including information technology, social sciences, marketing and management. She is interested in relationships, networks and values. She has written articles in internationally published research magazines and in books.

BOOKS BY A.T. SORSA

YA and Children Fiction:
Animellis Island Book One: The Traitor Gator
Animellis Island Book Two: Up, Up, and Away!

Children Picture Book:
What Is Causing the Scary Nighttime Sounds?

Quick Help Books for Children, Tweens, and Teens:
Bullies and Bullied
Time Management for Girls
Time Management for Boys

Quick Help Books for Parents:
How to Motivate Your Child

Made in the USA
Lexington, KY
30 March 2012